Sign Language
& Vehicles

Bela Davis

Abdo Kids Junior
is an Imprint of Abdo Kids
abdobooks.com

Abdo
EVERYDAY SIGN LANGUAGE
Kids

abdobooks.com

Published by Abdo Kids, a division of ABDO, P.O. Box 398166, Minneapolis, Minnesota 55439. Copyright © 2023 by Abdo Consulting Group, Inc. International copyrights reserved in all countries. No part of this book may be reproduced in any form without written permission from the publisher. Abdo Kids Junior™ is a trademark and logo of Abdo Kids.

Printed in the United States of America, North Mankato, Minnesota.

102022

012023

 THIS BOOK CONTAINS RECYCLED MATERIALS

Photo Credits: Getty Images, Shutterstock

Production Contributors: Teddy Borth, Jennie Forsberg, Grace Hansen

Design Contributors: Candice Keimig, Pakou Moua

Library of Congress Control Number: 2022937171

Publisher's Cataloging-in-Publication Data

Names: Davis, Bela, author.

Title: Sign language & vehicles / by Bela Davis

Description: Minneapolis, Minnesota : Abdo Kids, 2023 | Series: Everyday sign language | Includes online resources and index.

Identifiers: ISBN 9781098264109 (lib. bdg.) | ISBN 9781098264666 (ebook) | ISBN 9781098264949 (Read-to-Me ebook)

Subjects: LCSH: American Sign Language--Juvenile literature. | Vehicles--Juvenile literature. | Deaf--Means of communication--Juvenile literature. | Language acquisition--Juvenile literature.

Classification: DDC 419--dc23

Table of Contents

Signs and Vehicles

ASL is a visual language. There is a sign for every vehicle!

VEHICLE

1. Make the "3" sign
2. Hold the hand up with the pinky closest to the ground
3. Move hand away from the body in a straight line, like a vehicle would move down the road

Ed and Ned ride their bikes.

BIKE

1. Hold "S" hands in front of the body with palms facing down
2. Pedal the fists, making them move like feet moving the pedals of a bicycle

Willow helps her dad
wash the car.

CAR

1. Hold two "S" hands out in front of the body with palms facing each other
2. Alternate moving the fists up and down in a slightly rounded motion
3. It should look like holding and moving the steering wheel of a car

The big truck drives down
the road.

TRUCK

1. Fingerspell T-R-U-C-K

The school bus is long
and yellow.

B U S

BUS

1. Fingerspell B-U-S

The tiny **rubber** boats

float in the tub.

BOAT

1. Using both hands, make a boat shape with palms facing up

2. Move the hands up and down while extending them forward as if showing the movement of a boat over water

The train moves along
the **track**.

TRAIN

1. Using both hands, extend the pointer and middle fingers while tucking the others in

2. Take the dominant hand and move the fingers back and forth down the same fingers on the non-dominant hand

3. It is like the fingers are a train moving down a track

The airplane flies high
in the sky.

AIRPLANE

1. Take an outstretched hand and tuck in the middle and ring fingers

2. Then move the hand away from the body a short distance while bobbing it back and forth a couple of times, as if it is flying.

Rory pretends he's on a rocket ship to space!

ROCKET

1. Hold up the non-dominant hand vertically and in front of the body

2. Sign the letter "R" with the dominant hand

3. Hold the "R" hand parallel with the other hand and launch the "R" hand like a rocket up into space

The ASL Alphabet!

Glossary

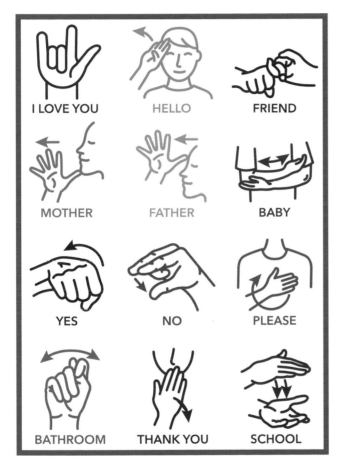

ASL

short for American Sign Language, a language used by many deaf people in North America.

rubber

a strong, stretchy solid made of natural or man-made materials.

track

a pair of connected rails on which trains travel.

Index

Abdo Kids ONLINE
FREE! ONLINE MULTIMEDIA RESOURCES

Visit **abdokids.com** to access crafts, games, videos, and more!

Use Abdo Kids code

ESK4109

or scan this QR code!